AWESOME FORCES OF NATURE

SWEEPING TSUNAMIS

Revised and Updated

Louise and Richard Spilsbury

Heinemann
LIBRARY
Chicago, Illinois

www.heinemannraintree.com
Visit our website to find out
more information about
Heinemann-Raintree books.

To order:

☎ Phone 888-454-2279

🖥 Visit www.heinemannraintree.com
to browse our catalog and order online.

Edited by Megan Cotugno, Abby Colich, and Andrew Farrow
Designed by Richard Parker
Original illustrations © Capstone Global Library 2004
Illustrated by Geoff Ward
Picture research by Hannah Taylor
Production by Alison Parsons
Originated by Capstone Global Library, Ltd.
Printed and bound in China by Leo Paper Products, Ltd.

13 12 11 10
10 9 8 7 6 5 4 3 2 1

Library of Congress Cataloging-in-Publication Data

Spilsbury, Louise.
  Sweeping tsunamis / Louise and Richard Spilsbury.
    p. cm. -- (Awesome forces of nature)
  Includes bibliographical references and index.
  ISBN 978-1-4329-3785-0 (hc) -- ISBN 978-1-4329-3792-
8 (pb) 1. Tsunamis--Juvenile literature. 2. Tsunamis--
Environmental aspects--Juvenile literature. I. Spilsbury,
Richard, 1963- II. Title.
  GC221.5. S69 2010
  551.46'37--dc22
                    2009037567

Acknowledgements
We would like to thank the following for permission to
reproduce photographs: Corbis: 7 (Charles O'Rear), 22
(Reuters/Simon Kwong), 27 (Wolfgang Kaehler); EPA: 9 (Mike
Nelson); Getty Images: 4 (AFP), 17 (AFP/John Russell), 18
(AFP/Raveendran), 19 (AFP), 20 (AFP/Jewel Samad); NOAA:
11, 15, 26; Reuters: 14 (Enny Nuraheni); Rex Features: 5 (Sipa
Press), 12 (Sipa Press), 21, 28 (Sipa Press); Science Photo
Library: 23 (Eurelios/LDG/Carlos Munoz-Yague), 25 (Tony
Craddock); Te Papa Tongarewa Museum of New Zealand: 24.

Cover photograph of a devastated beach in Khao Lak,
Thailand, after the tsunami disaster in 2004, reproduced with
permission of Rex Features (Lewis Whyld).

We would like to thank Dr. Ramesh Srivastava for his
invaluable help in the preparation of this book.

Every effort has been made to contact copyright holders of
material reproduced in this book. Any omissions will be
rectified in subsequent printings if notice is given to the
publishers.

All the Internet addresses (URLs) given in this book were valid
at the time of going to press. However, due to the dynamic
nature of the Internet, some addresses may have changed, or
sites may have changed or ceased to exist since publication.
While the author and publisher regret any inconvenience this
may cause readers, no responsibility for any such changes can
be accepted by either the author or the publisher.

Contents

Any words appearing in the text in bold, **like this**, are explained in the glossary.

What Is a Tsunami?

A tsunami is a huge destructive ocean wave. It is nothing like an ordinary wave. As ocean waves move into shallow water, their narrow foaming tips curl over and "break" (collapse). A tsunami hits land as a dark, fast-moving ledge of water that rarely breaks as it nears shore. Most tsunamis are barely noticeable in deep parts of oceans, but they get bigger as they approach land.

TSUNAMI FACTS

❶ The biggest tsunamis are the most destructive waves on the planet.

❷ The fastest tsunamis in the world can reach speeds of 800 kilometers (497 miles) per hour.

❸ Tsunamis have reached heights of 40 meters (131 feet) above the normal level of the sea.

Big tsunamis may move toward the land at hundreds of kilometers per hour. This photo, of a first tsunami wave, was taken by a tourist on the island of Penang, Malaysia, in December 2004.

Awesome force

Big tsunamis are like huge walls of water. They can be tens of meters tall and several kilometers wide, containing millions of tons of water. The water smacks hard onto land with the same force as a wall of concrete.

Anything in the way of a big tsunami—from people to giant ships or trucks—may be swept away, crushed, or buried under water. Trees and telephone poles are snapped like matchsticks. Homes, schools, and lighthouses may collapse as if made of cardboard. Over the past 100 years, tsunamis have killed hundreds of thousands of people and caused millions of dollars worth of damage around the world.

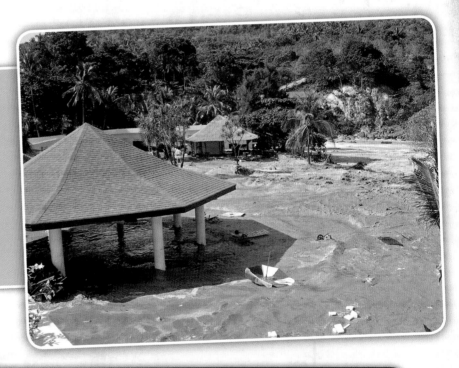

The 2004 Indian Ocean tsunami caused flooding on Koh Racha Island, in Thailand. This luxury hotel was destroyed by three large waves.

Harbor waves

Tsunami is a Japanese word that means "harbor wave." It was given this name because of the great devastation caused around the coastal harbors of Japan by many tsunamis.

What Causes a Tsunami?

Tsunamis usually happen when giant chunks of land at the bottom of the ocean move as the result of an **earthquake**. Millions of tons of seawater move in to fill the gap. This causes a series of waves on the surface of the ocean—a bit like the ripples that spread out when you drop a stone into a pond or lake.

Earth movements

The outer layer of the Earth is made of solid rock. On mountain tops, it can be bare, on deserts it may be covered with sand, and in oceans it is covered with seawater. Incredibly, this rock is always moving, although it does this very slowly. Deep inside the Earth, it is so hot that the rock is melted into a sticky liquid. The cooler, lighter rock of the surface floats around on top of this liquid in enormous chunks called **plates**.

The Earth's plates

ocean

crust

land

hot, soft rock inside Earth

cool, hard rock of outer layer forming plates

As the Earth's plates move, they push and slide against each other. Sometimes the plates stick and then one suddenly slips, causing an earthquake.

Other causes of tsunamis

All tsunamis start when massive amounts of seawater are suddenly moved. Sometimes the **lava** in the Earth spurts out at gaps or thin spots in the plates. This is what we call a **volcano**. When underwater volcanoes explode, they destroy rocks around them and this can start tsunamis.

Tsunamis can also be started when large amounts of rock or ice on mountains suddenly break free and fall into water. Tsunamis could even happen if a large meteorite (a piece of rock from space) plunged into an ocean.

In 1883 the Krakatoa volcano in Indonesia erupted. The whole island collapsed and caused 35-meter (115-foot) high tsunamis that sped toward neighboring islands, killing 36,000 people.

Deep beginnings

Tsunamis move outward from the point where they start. Imagine you are on a plane flying over an ocean. If an **earthquake** struck hundreds of meters below on the **seafloor**, all you would see is crumpled water for an instant. The sea would then flatten again and a tsunami would speed away.

Tsunamis travel fastest in deep water. The **crest** of a tsunami in deep water may be only one meter (three feet) tall. This crest is just the tip of a deep wave that reaches tens of meters into the water. As the wave moves toward shallower water, its bottom slows down as it touches the seafloor, but the top pushes forward at speed. The water then bunches up, and the tsunami is at its tallest as it reaches the coast.

Tsunamis can build to great heights as they get closer to land. Although they slow down, they can still hit coastlines at hundreds of kilometers per hour.

How tsunamis reach land

③ waves slow up and pile up toward land

④ tsunami reaches land

① seafloor slips down after earthquake

② sudden change in depth of seafloor starts tsunami

Enormous forces

Tsunamis shift immense quantities of water at such speed that they can travel over very long distances. In 1960 an earthquake off Chile in South America started a tsunami. The tsunami traveled 15,000 kilometers (9,321 miles) in 22 hours before hitting the coast of Japan. A big tsunami is barely slowed down when it flows over a small island, but it usually stops after it hits a **continent**. Some large tsunamis bounce back off continents and move back and forth over whole oceans, getting gradually weaker, over several days.

Tsunamis and tidal waves

Tsunamis are sometimes wrongly called tidal waves. Tidal waves are waves caused by **tides**. Tides are the regular rise and fall of the level of the oceans, caused by the pull of **gravity** of the moon and the sun. Especially high tides sometimes cause large tidal waves, but never tsunamis.

After the first tsunami waves, weaker waves continue to hit the mainland, adding to the damage. Here, the town of Hakkaduwa in Sri Lanka is being hit by the later waves of the 2004 Indian Ocean tsunami.

Where Do Tsunamis Happen?

Most tsunamis happen in the Pacific Ocean. Some of the countries most at risk from tsunamis are Japan, the U.S., Papua New Guinea, and Chile, because they border the Pacific. Tsunamis happen here because a part of the Earth's outer surface, called the Pacific **plate**, lies underneath the Pacific Ocean. There are lots of **earthquakes** and **volcanoes** along the edges of this plate, where it meets other plates. This area is often called the "Ring of Fire."

Where else do they happen?

Tsunamis affect other coasts where earthquakes happen in the ocean. They have hit countries in the Indian Ocean, Canada, which is at the edge of the Atlantic Ocean, and countries in the Mediterranean Sea.

The Ring of Fire

RUSSIA

Alaska

CANADA

San Francisco

USA

Los Angeles

Tokyo

JAPAN

Hawaii

PAPUA NEW GUINEA

INDONESIA

PACIFIC OCEAN

AUSTRALIA

CHILE

NEW ZEALAND

KEY
||| Ring of Fire

The countries around the edge of the Pacific Ocean are all at risk from tsunamis. But certain Pacific islands, such as Hawaii, are at a greater risk because they are in the middle of the Ring of Fire. Tsunamis can approach from all sides!

Shape of the land

Some parts of coasts are more affected by tsunamis than others. Towns and villages in greatest danger are those at **sea level** less than two kilometers (one mile) from the sea. Even quite small tsunamis can travel a long way over flat land like this.

Tsunamis are also dangerous in curved bays or at the end of **fjords** (river valleys with steep sides). The waves get very high between their narrow sides. When tsunamis reach **headlands**, which are narrow strips of land sticking out to sea, they wrap around it. Then water floods onto land from both sides.

TSUNAMI FACT

The highest tsunami ever recorded happened in Lituya Bay in Alaska in 1958. A **landslide** fell into the narrow fjord, causing a wave over 500 meters (1,640 feet) high—that's nearly as tall as the CN tower in Canada!

Tsunamis can roll much further inland over a flat coastline like this than over a steep or hilly shore.

What Happens in a Tsunami?

Tsunamis move very fast. If someone sees one approaching, then it is probably too late for him or her to get away from it! Sometimes, though, there are signs that a tsunami is on its way.

Many tsunami survivors describe how the **sea level** drops. Water is suddenly sucked away from the shore, uncovering sand, mud, and reefs on the sea floor and leaving fish and boats stranded. The reason for this is that the water has moved to fill the space on the ocean floor created by an **earthquake**. Then the water returns in waves.

> " *I saw the entire bay suddenly drain of water with a quiet roar.*
>
> —Mark Vanderkam, a survivor of the tsunami that hit Thailand in 2004 "

Before the first tsunami waves arrive, the sea is sucked back from the shore. This is what it looked like at Galle in Sri Lanka right before the 2004 tsunami hit.

Wave train

As the sea gurgles out from land, there is sometimes a very strong wind. This is air being pushed in front of the speeding tsunami. A big tsunami often comes in a series of waves called a wave train. The time between each wave **crest** may be minutes or even as long as an hour. Between each tsunami crest there is a **trough**, when water is again sucked out to sea. It seems like the water is being pulled by an enormous vacuum cleaner before it shoots back!

The first tsunami wave to break may not cause the most damage. Other, more damaging waves may arrive later.

The first tsunami may not be the worst—the biggest, most dangerous waves in a wave train are often the third and eighth waves to arrive. After the tsunamis have struck, it may take days before normal ocean waves get back to their expected sizes.

13

Destruction

A big tsunami can destroy almost anything in its path. In an instant, whole areas of homes, farms, and factories may be ruined. Many animals and people may be drowned under meters of water, or carried up to a kilometer (a half mile) inland. Cars, trains, boats, buses, shattered buildings, and bridges are carried inland at high speed, like missiles. They may crush other things in their way.

The whole of a coastline may be altered by a tsunami. The seawater may flood large areas of low-lying land, ruining farmers' **crops**. Trees, other plants, and soil are sometimes stripped from the land, and the sucking action of the wave train may shift whole beaches.

Tsunamis can cause horrific devastation. Whole cities were flattened as a result of the Indian Ocean tsunami in late December 2004. This was the city of Banda Aceh in Indonesia.

After the waves

When a tsunami is over, daily life does not return to normal for some time. Many people, such as fishermen with broken boats, cannot earn money because they cannot work. Children may not be able to go to school. There are many health hazards. Drinking water and **sewage** get mixed with seawater when pipes are snapped and **reservoirs** broken. People may then drink **polluted** water containing germs that will make them ill. Many are at risk of **electrocution** from damaged **powerlines**. Sometimes gas that leaks from broken pipes explodes.

When the seawater drains away, massive amounts of **debris** left on land have to be cleared up. Some debris comes from collapsed buildings or trees. Other debris is from the ocean—tsunamis pick up tons of sand, coral, rock, and fish as they approach land.

Tsunami waters left tons of debris and dead fish on the beaches of Banda Aceh, Indonesia, after the 2004 tsunami disaster.

CASE STUDY

The Indian Ocean, 2004

On the morning of December 26, 2004, a huge **earthquake** shook the seabed off the Indonesian island of Sumatra. A tsunami sped away across the Indian Ocean, traveling at speeds of 480 kilometers (298 miles) an hour. The thousands of people who were working, playing, and relaxing on the coasts of eight countries had no idea the tsunami was coming. Their only warning was when the sea suddenly pulled back hundreds of meters from the shore. The first wave caught most people unaware. Indonesia, Sri Lanka, Thailand, and India were hit the hardest. Nearly 230,000 people died.

> " *A great wave came rushing into the shore, destroying everything and sweeping away everybody who was in the way. Everyone vanished in a second. The whole town was destroyed, along with people at the bus stand and vehicles on the road.*
>
> —Deepa, a Sri Lankan survivor "

The circles on this map show how the earthquake that began near Indonesia caused a tsunami that traveled as far as the coast of East Africa.

Damage

Many people were injured and thousands of homes, hotels, and businesses were destroyed. Countries as far away as the Maldives and Somalia were affected. The costs of **aid**, clearing up, and rebuilding were in the region of $7 billion. The rest of the world was shocked by the scale of the disaster and money flooded in to help victims and restore basic services.

After this disaster, **scientists** called for a tsunami early warning system around the Indian Ocean, like the one in the Pacific Ocean. Next time warning sirens could be sounded to give people a chance to escape to a safer place.

TSUNAMI FACTS

❶ The 2004 tsunami took fifteen minutes to reach Indonesia and seven hours to reach Somalia.

❷ Many victims drowned picking up fish flung on to the beach by the first waves.

People ran for their lives when the tsunami hit the shore of Koh Raya, Thailand, in 2004.

17

Who Helps When Tsunamis Happen?

Many people help the victims of tsunamis. **Scientists** tell coast guards and government officials if there has been an **earthquake** that might start a tsunami. Then fire, police, and ambulance services, and the navy are put on alert. Hospitals prepare to treat tsunami victims.

Authorities use radio and TV **broadcasts** to warn people that they may have to **evacuate**. They might also visit people where they live to tell them. If a tsunami is definitely on its way, sirens may be sounded so that people know they must evacuate to a safe place. Most people can travel on their own, but some young, old, or sick people need help evacuating. The police and army usually help organize evacuations.

Local authorities and charities such as the Red Cross give first aid to injured people. They also collect food and water supplies and organize shelter for evacuated people.

Emergency help

More help is needed if a tsunami happens unexpectedly, or if it
affects more land than expected. Emergency services find and rescue
people washed out to sea or trapped in dangerous places such as
boats or unsafe buildings. Fire services put out fires of spilled oil or gas.
Paramedics and doctors give **first aid** for injuries such as wounds and
broken bones.

In some poorer countries, emergency services may not be able to cope
with a tsunami disaster. They will ask for **aid** from other governments
and international organizations and **charities**. Many of these groups
may also help over a longer period, working with local people to rebuild
homes and hospitals. In places where farms have been destroyed, they
give seeds and **livestock** so people can feed themselves again. They
also give new pipes and pumps to provide a safe water supply.

What to do when a tsunami happens

- People who live or work on the coast should move two to three kilometers (one to two miles) inland or to higher ground.
- People on a boat on deep sea should stay there and not return to land. The height of waves is lower further out to sea, over deep water.
- People should keep a radio or telephone nearby to listen for further warnings and messages.
- People should never return to a tsunami-hit area until they are told the waves have stopped coming.
- People should keep away from buildings left standing after a tsunami, because they might collapse.

People on boats near coasts should head out to sea if they hear a tsunami warning. Boats near the coast will be tossed and smashed onto the land like toys, like this boat in Banda Aceh, Indonesia, in 2004.

CASE STUDY

Japan, 1993

On July 12, 1993, an **earthquake** struck 20 kilometers (12 miles) off the island of Okushiri. The Japanese authorities gave a tsunami warning on radio and TV within 5 minutes, so many people were able to **evacuate** to higher ground. However, waves 5 to 30 meters (16 to 98 feet) high had already struck Aonae, a fishing village on Okushiri's southern **headland**. Over 200 were killed by the waves.

The Japan Maritime Safety Agency used helicopters, boats, and divers to find missing people. Heavy cranes and bulldozers were used to clear **debris** that had filled the harbor.

The sports hall of Aonae Middle School became a temporary shelter for hundreds of people whose homes were destroyed. Their new homes were built farther away from the sea, so any future tsunamis would affect them less.

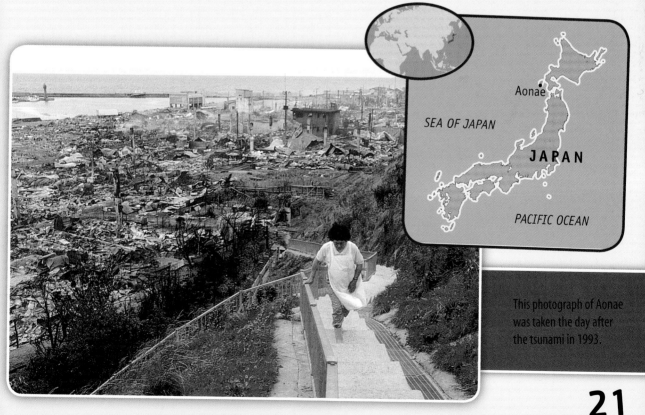

Aonae

SEA OF JAPAN

J A P A N

PACIFIC OCEAN

This photograph of Aonae was taken the day after the tsunami in 1993.

Can Tsunamis Be Predicted?

Scientists around the world work together to predict tsunamis. They use machines called **seismographs** to record when and where **earthquakes** strike and how strong they are. If a big earthquake happens under or near an ocean, the scientists warn neighboring countries that it may cause a tsunami. However, not every earthquake starts a tsunami, so scientists have developed ways of detecting and tracking tsunamis.

Detecting waves

There is a network of special research stations around the Pacific Ocean that measures the heights of **tides**. Scientists use these stations to notice sudden changes in water level that happen before a tsunami. Scientists from Japan and the U.S. have laid cables on the ocean floor, near their coasts. Special boxes along the cables sense when a deep tsunami wave passes over them. The boxes send this information via **satellites** to scientists onshore, so that they know a tsunami is on its way.

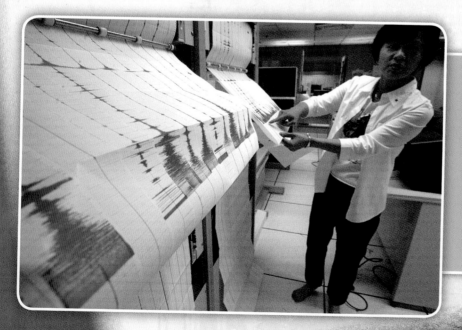

The marks on this paper show Earth movements recorded by a seismograph. The more the ground shakes, the bigger an earthquake is.

Looking into the future

Many countries use powerful computers to help them **simulate** how tsunamis will affect their coasts. To do this, they prepare special electronic maps of coastal places, showing where people live, and what the land around is like—for example, if it is flat or hilly. They also put in information about previous tsunamis, such as how far they travel on flat land and up steeper slopes. They then simulate different sizes and speeds of tsunamis hitting these places.

Simulations like this are vital to work out the best places to **evacuate** people. Local authorities can then tell people the quickest escape routes if a tsunami approaches. Simulations also show people where the safest places to build are.

These are computer simulations of tsunamis hitting land. They give people a good idea of what might happen if a tsunami were to hit their coast.

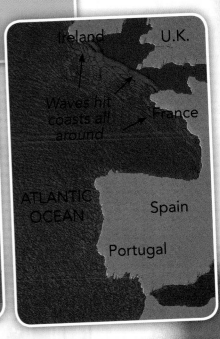

Can People Prepare for Tsunamis?

People who live in places threatened by tsunamis must understand the danger they are in. They can then prepare in various ways, from the way they build their houses to knowing how to **evacuate**.

Building for tsunamis

The damage caused by tsunamis can be reduced if buildings are made stronger. For example, most of the repair costs after the Aonae tsunami (see page 21) were spent fixing damaged harbor walls. Since then new, taller, strengthened sea walls have been built around parts of Japan. In Hawaii many office and hotel buildings are now designed on stilts—the ground floor is open parking space with rooms above. The water should then pass through the open space and not damage the building structure.

This museum in New Zealand is shaped so that waves can move around it. It is also built on special rubber feet so waves can move it 75 centimeters (30 inches) without damaging it.

Evacuation plans

It is vital for people to know the best way of getting themselves, their family, pets, and farm animals to a safe place. All family members should know how to contact each other or where to meet if they are not all in the same place. They should also know things about where they live and understand evacuation warnings. People should always take evacuation warnings seriously. They should also look out for tsunami signs such as sudden changes in **sea level**.

A tsunami survival kit

If people have to evacuate, they should take the following:

- a **first-aid** kit and any essential medicines
- enough food and water for at least three days
- a flashlight and radio with extra batteries
- warm clothing, blankets, or sleeping bags
- money and important papers such as passport and driver's license.

States bordering the Pacific Ocean have put up tsunami signs like this, which show people the way they should go if they hear a tsunami warning on the radio or television.

Papua New Guinea, 1998

In July 1998, an **earthquake** started a giant underwater **landslide** that caused an immense tsunami. It was dusk when three huge waves swept over Arop and other villages around Sissano lagoon in northern Papua New Guinea.

Earthquakes are common in Papua New Guinea because it is near the join between of two of the Earth's **plates**. However, most of the local people did not know about tsunamis. A rumble was heard out at sea and many people moved closer to see the sea drawing back and then rising above the horizon. Those who could ran for their lives. The first wave flooded the land and broke up the villagers' flimsy wooden houses. The second wave, which was 10 meters (33 feet) high, swept everything away in front of it. Two whole villages were completely destroyed. Thousands of people were injured or killed, many by being thrown against trees or being hit by floating **debris**. Many of the victims were children.

Sissano

PAPUA
NEW GUINEA

PACIFIC OCEAN

Before

After

These pictures show a village center before and after the tsunami of 1998. Whole buildings were wiped out by the tsunami's awesome power.

Future safety

After the disaster, Australian emergency services and **charities** such as Oxfam worked with the government of Papua New Guinea to look after survivors. They provided **aid** and helped them rebuild their lives. They also showed local people what to do if another tsunami happened.

Charity workers and the government of Papua New Guinea produced posters, leaflets, special TV programs, and videos about tsunamis. They took these to all the coastal villages and told local people what to do if a tsunami happens. In November 2000 another, smaller, tsunami struck, but amazingly no one was killed. Most people had remembered their lessons. They had climbed to high ground as soon as the earth began to shake and the **sea level** changed.

In Papua New Guinea, children are now taught all about tsunamis at school. Teachers explain that Papua New Guinea has been hit by many earthquakes and tsunamis, and tell the children what to do if a tsunami happens.

Can Tsunamis Be Prevented?

Tsunamis are natural events that have happened throughout the history of the Earth. Just as we cannot stop **earthquakes** or **volcanoes**, we cannot prevent tsunamis. There has been at least one tsunami a year in the Pacific Ocean since 1800, and there will be more in the future. Big tsunamis that affect the coasts of many countries happen about once every seven to ten years.

Changing world

As the population of the world grows, coastal towns and cities get bigger. This means that each tsunami may affect more people. Some states have areas of sand and gravel on their coast. These were dropped there by big tsunamis in the past when few people lived there. If a big tsunami happened now, millions of people on the Pacific coast might be affected.

Seismographs such as the one shown here can help seismologists learn more about tsunamis.

Sweeping Tsunamis of the Past

Lisbon, Portugal, 1775
An earthquake and tsunami killed over 100,00 people.

Calabria, Italy, 1908
After an earthquake, a 15-meter (49-foot) high tsunami killed almost 100,000 people.

Sanriku, Japan, 1933
An earthquake created a tsunami that killed 3,000 people, broke 9,000 buildings, and overturned 8,000 boats. The waves were felt as far away as Iquique, Chile.

Hilo, Hawaii, 1946
A tsunami struck killing over 100 people. This event led to the development of an early warning system in the Pacific Ocean by the U.S. government.

Alaska, 1957
This Pacific-wide tsunami damaged coasts in Alaska, British Columbia, Washington, Oregon, California, and the Hawaiian Islands. Waves were as high as 23 meters (75 feet). It killed 156 people.

Chile, 1960
One of the most destructive Pacific-wide tsunamis, this tsunami, caused by an earthquake, created waves up to 25 meters (82 feet) high. In Chile thousands of people died and about 2,000,000 were left homeless as a result of the tsunami and the earthquake. The tsunami also killed 61 people in Hawaii.

San Juan Island, Colombia, 1979
A tsunami destroyed all homes on the island and killed 250 people.

Japan, 1993
A tsunami with waves of up to 31 meters (102 feet) high hit the Japanese island of Hokkaido. It killed 239 people, but early warning systems prevented even greater disaster.

Papua New Guinea, 1998
A tsunami caused by an earthquake off the northern coast of Papua New Guinea killed 2,182 people, injured 1,000, and left 10,000 homeless.

Indian Ocean, 2004
An earthquake off the Indonesian island of Sumatra created a tsunami that caused the death of about 230,000 people. Indonesia, Thailand, India, and Sri Lanka were worst hit but the waves traveled as far as Somalia in East Africa.

Glossary

aid help given as money, medicine, food, or other essential items

broadcast program (on radio or TV) that gives information to many people

charity organization that gives out aid and makes people aware of disasters

continent seven large land masses on Earth—Asia, Africa, North America, South America, Europe, Australia, and Antarctica

crest highest point

crop plant grown by people for food or other uses

debris broken pieces of buildings, trees, rocks, etc.

earthquake shaking of the ground caused by large movements inside the Earth

electrocution when someone is injured by electricity

evacuate move away from danger until it is safe to return

first aid first medical help given to injured people

fjord narrow strip of sea between high cliffs

gravity force that attracts objects together and which holds us on the ground

headland strip of land sticking out into the sea

landslide when a large piece of land suddenly slides down a slope

lava melted rock from inside the Earth that comes out of a volcano

livestock animals kept by people to eat or to sell

paramedic medical worker who travels to where an accident has happened to help people

plate sheet of rock that forms part of the surface of the Earth

polluted when air, soil, or water is poisoned or dirtied

powerlines cables that carry electricity

reservoir large natural or manmade lake used to collect and store water

satellite object made by humans and put into space. Satellites do jobs such as sending out TV signals or taking photographs.

scientist person who studies aspects of the world around us

sea level normal level of the sea's surface and land that is at the same level

seafloor solid bottom of a sea or ocean

seismograph machine that records the force and direction of an earthquake

sewage waste matter from toilets and drains

simulate to show accurately how something would happen

tide regular rise and fall of the oceans

trough a wave's trough is its lowest level

volcano hole in the Earth's surface through which lava, hot gases, smoke, and ash escape

Find Out More

Books

Langley, Andrew. *Hurricanes, Tsunamis, and Other Natural Disasters.* (New York: Kingfisher, 2006).

Tagliaferro, Linda. *How Does an Earthquake Become a Tsunami?* (Chicago: Raintree, 2009).

Townsend, John. *The Asian Tsunami 2004.* (Chicago: Raintree, 2006).

Websites

FEMA for Kids
www.fema.gov/kids/tsunami.htm
This website gives facts about tsunami dangers, including what to do and how to prepare.

Pacific Tsunami Museum
www.tsunami.org/students.html
The website of the Pacific Tsunami Museum, which has photos and stories of tsunamis in the past.

Tsunami!
www.ess.washington.edu/tsunami/index.html
This website by the University of Washington provides lots of information about tsunamis.

Index